American pop culture

Art

Jil Fine

Children's Press®
A Division of Scholastic Inc.
New York / Toronto / London / Auckland / Sydney
Mexico City / New Delhi / Hong Kong
Danbury, Connecticut

Book Design: Michael DeLisio and Mindy Liu
Contributing Editor: Matt Pitt
Photo Credits: Cover © 2003 Andy Warhol Foundation /ARS, NY/ TM Licensed by Campbell's Soup Co. All rights reserved, photo © Burstein Collection/Corbis; p. 4 © 2003 Andy Warhol Foundation for the Visual Arts/ARS, New York, photo Art Resource, NY; p. 7 Art © The George and Helen Segal Foundation/Licensed by VAGA, New York, NY, photo © AP/Wide World Photos; p. 8 © The Newark Museum/Art Resource, NY; p. 11 © 2003 Artists Rights Society (ARS), New York/ ADAGP, Paris/Succession Marcel Duchamp, photo © Cameraphoto/Art Resource, NY; p. 16 © 1998 Kate Rothko Prizel & Christopher Rothko/Artists Rights Society (ARS), New York, photo © Art Resource, NY; p. 19 © 2003 The Pollock-Krasner Foundation/Artists Rights Society (ARS), New York, photo © Giraudon/Art Resource, NY; pp. 20, 27, 29, 34, 37, 38 © AP/Wide World Photos; pp. 22 Art by Robert Rauschenberg © Robert Rauschenberg/Licensed by VAGA, New York, NY, photo © Richard Schulman/Corbis; p. 24 © Richard Shulman/Corbis; p. 30 © 2003 Andy Warhol Foundation for the Visual Arts/ARS, New York, photo © Digital Image ©The Museum of Modern Art/Licensed by Scala/Art Resource, NY; p. 33 © Estate of Roy Lichtenstein, photo © Tate Gallery, London/Art Resource, NY; p. 40 Courtesy: Mary Boone Gallery, New York, photo © Christie's Images/Corbis

Library of Congress Cataloging-in-Publication Data

Fine, Jil.
  Art / by Jil Fine.
  p. cm.—(American pop culture)
  Includes index.
  Summary: An overview of trends in the visual arts in America, in the context of popular culture, from the twentieth century until today.
  ISBN 0-516-24073-0 (lib. bdg.)—ISBN 0-516-25942-3 (pbk.)
  1. Art and popular culture—United States—Juvenile literature. [1. Art. 2. Popular culture—United States.] I. Title. II. Series.

N72.S6F554 2004
306.4'7'0973—dc22

2003015395

Copyright © 2004 by Rosen Book Works, Inc. All rights reserved.
Published in 2004 by Children's Press, an imprint of
Scholastic Library Publishing.
Published simultaneously in Canada.
Printed in China.

CHILDREN'S PRESS and associated logos are trademarks and or registered trademarks of Scholastic Library Publishing. SCHOLASTIC and associated logos are trademarks and or registered trademarks of Scholastic Inc.

3 4 5 6 7 8 9 10 R 13 12 11 10 09 08 07

Contents

	Introduction	5
1	New Century, New Canvas	9
2	Art Defining America	17
3	Eye-Popping Art	25
4	Pop Art Echoes On	35
	New Words	42
	For Further Reading	44
	Resources	45
	Index	47
	About the Author	48

Paintings such as this one, by famous and wildly successful pop artists, have turned buying and selling artwork into a huge business.

Introduction

You and your class are on a field trip. You are spending the day in a museum of modern art. The museum is filled with colorful artwork. In every room, amazing paintings, sculptures, and photographs await your view. Each piece of art has been made by an American artist. You walk into a room featuring one piece of art. It's a painting of the film actress Marilyn Monroe. Her hair is bright yellow. Her face has been painted pale, purplish pink. Behind her is a burnt orange background.

"This piece is called *Shot Orange Marilyn*," the museum guide announces to your class. "It recently sold at an auction for over 17 million dollars." Your jaw drops in surprise. How could a single painting be worth so much money? After all, you saw a poster of Marilyn Monroe in a store several weeks ago. It only cost *seventeen* dollars.

You keep walking through the museum. As you stroll from room to room, the wide range of styles and subject matter startles and impresses you. There are paintings of soup cans next to a papier-mâché flashlight. One painting looks like a panel from a comic strip. There's sculpture of bronze cans. On the wall next to that, there's a stunning photo of an eggbeater.

A few weeks before taking this field trip, you had read about the 1893 World's Fair in Chicago. In 1893, America was still very young. The fair was meant to display the culture and power this new nation had already achieved. Statues, buildings, and artwork were created for the event. However, these creations didn't have much of an American style. In fact, many of the artists borrowed from Greek, Roman, and French styles.

You may wonder how art's most popular styles could have changed so much in such a short time. How did we go from painting rural landscapes to comic strips? At the 1893 Chicago World's Fair, one artist created a statue

Portrait of Sidney Janis with Mondrian Painting by George Segal, Art © The George and Helen Segal Foundation/ Licensed by VAGA, New York, NY

The works of George Segal are certainly eye catching. However, his style has little in common with that of nineteenth-century sculptors.

of a giant golden goddess. Just seventy years later, artist George Segal created a famous sculpture of a woman shaving her legs.

World events and the artists' personal experiences help to keep art fresh and surprising. New styles may react to, or rebel against, older ones. Styles may change from year to year, but popular art continues to be an important part of American culture.

In the early twentieth century, The Eight made a big splash by painting busy scenes of city life. This 1907 John Sloan painting shows a crowd gathering around a shop window.

New Century, New Canvas

The Eight

In February 1908, a group of eight talented American artists were unhappy with the artwork being shown at museums. They felt that too much of American artwork was created by and for a select group of people. They decided to hold a private art show in New York City.

The group called themselves The Eight. They tried to capture the reality of rapidly growing cities in their work. They didn't shy away from showing crowds, crime, or poverty. They believed this was an honest reflection of city life.

Some artists used quick brush strokes to give their paintings energy. Their artwork was raw and vivid. It wasn't as polished as earlier American paintings. Other members of The Eight painted portraits of people. However, they refused to paint only portraits of wealthy people, which was the style at that time.

The art created by The Eight often brought attention to things that were wrong in society. One piece that may have enraged one viewer made another laugh out loud. Some people disliked the paintings The Eight created. They called the group Ashcan artists. That's because their work was filled with gritty details like garbage cans. Other people loved the work. They believed that more Americans could enjoy and appreciate this new type of art. The Eight appeared in newspapers and magazines across the United States.

Marcel's Marvel

In 1914, World War I began in Europe. Many European artists came to America to avoid the war's destruction. One of those artists was a Frenchman named Marcel Duchamp.

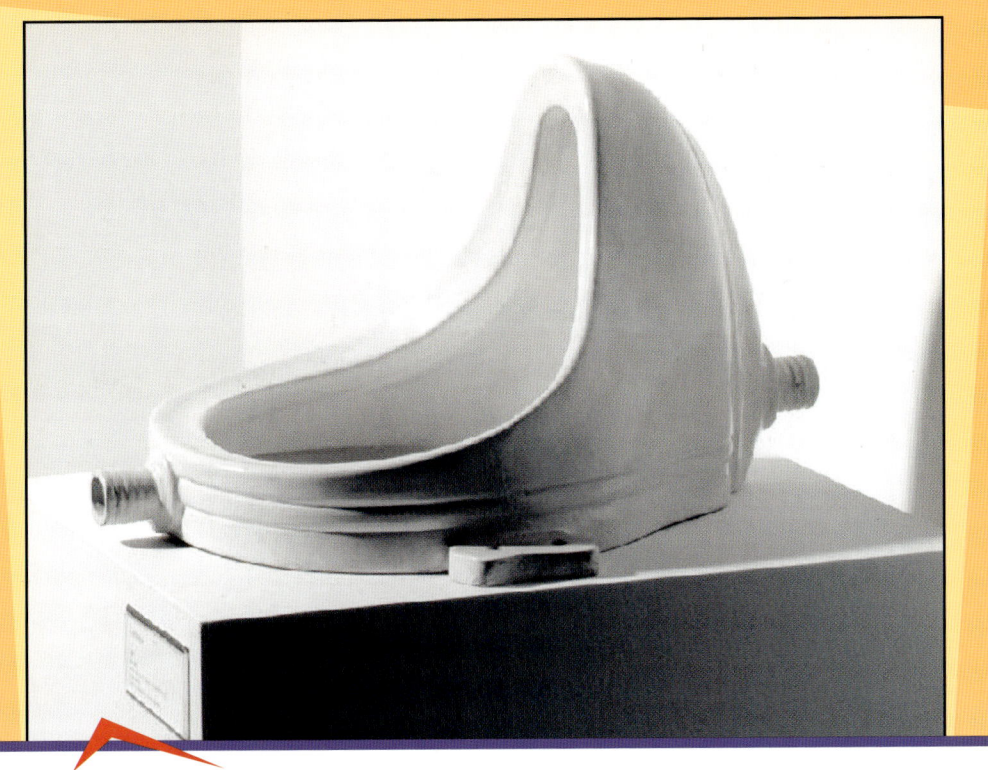

Marcel Duchamp didn't even sign his own name to his most famous work. Instead, he wrote the alias "R. Mutt" on a side of the urinal.

Duchamp helped organize The Big Show of the Society of Independent Artists. This art show opened in New York City, in April 1917. The Big Show was to be non-juried. This meant that there were no rules over what art could be entered.

Duchamp submitted an unusual piece of art. It was a urinal that he had bought at a plumbing supply company. Duchamp turned the urinal sideways, signed it, and called it *Fountain*. Then he submitted it as a piece of art.

Art

When the Society's directors saw *Fountain*, they refused to allow it in the show. Duchamp had found the limits of the American art world. He ended his membership in the Society. Before The Big Show, Duchamp hoped that American artists would blaze new trails and make their own traditions. "If only America would realize that the art of Europe is finished," he said. "America is the country of the art of the future!"

Duchamp was disappointed that his piece was rejected. Though he didn't realize it then, he was ahead of his time. While many critics chose to reject his ideas, the artists of the next generation would be listening. Duchamp's ideas and energy paved the way for American pop art.

Did You Know?

MORE THAN 2,100 PIECES OF ART WERE SUBMITTED AT THE BIG SHOW.

Many pop artists blur the line between fine art and mass culture. Pop art often uses images that can be found in everyday life. The images and objects of pop art may come from magazine ads or comic strips. They may be taken from photography or movie posters. They can be images of famous movie stars, or even Mickey Mouse. Like Duchamp, pop artists may simply take a household object and rename it as art.

Pop artists often borrow well-known images to create original pieces of art. Their artwork displays the familiar, but reflects it in an unusual way.

After the Great War

After World War I, the American economy began to grow. Factories sprang up across the nation. Washing machines, cars, and toasters were selling everywhere. Advertisements claimed that no one could live without these modern products. Many Americans began to believe such claims.

Some artists found inspiration in modern American industry. Charles Sheeler was hired

Art

to paint a picture celebrating Henry Ford's new automobile plant in Michigan. Charles Demuth's paintings also focused on American industry. However, some of Demuth's work also poked fun at people's devotion to business.

The Great Depression

In 1929, the stock market crashed. The Great Depression began. Factories and businesses went out of business. Millions of people lost their jobs and homes. Even those who kept their jobs were often forced to work for low wages.

Visual artists were also hit hard by the Great Depression. Many of them changed their approach to art. It no longer made sense to focus on painting skyscrapers and smokestacks. After all, many of those smokestacks had been shut down. A new style of art called social realism developed. Social realists created artwork that showed the problems that the nation faced. Some pieces of artwork called for society to change. Artists such as Reginald Marsh painted painful images of poor, hungry, and exhausted Americans.

In 1933, Franklin Roosevelt became president of the United States. Roosevelt knew he had to help those Americans hurt by the Great Depression. He started a program called the New Deal. The New Deal program helped many poor people get through tough times.

Roosevelt's New Deal also lent a hand to out-of-work artists. Many artists took pictures of Americans or painted murals in government buildings. Some artists were paid twenty-five dollars a week to make sculptures or paint posters.

Ben Shahn was a famous social realist. Shahn's work was concerned with justice and the problems of the times. One of his murals shows immigrants walking away from sweatshops and cramped apartments. Some critics suggested that the immigrants were walking toward the brighter future that the New Deal provided.

Often, Mark Rothko's work (pictured above) featured blocks of color on enormous canvases. Rothko was a major figure in the Abstract Expressionist movement.

Art Defining America

War-Torn World

On December 7, 1941, Japanese planes dropped bombs on Pearl Harbor, Hawaii. This attack marked the entry of the United States into World War II. The war lasted for nearly four long years. After the war was over, the United States prospered. It became the world's richest nation. It produced almost all of the world's cars. It also made more than half of the world's steel. Americans were urged to buy and sell large amounts of products. Spending and shopping soared. The population of the nation soared as well.

Art

Americans were living comfortably. However, many of them were also feeling great levels of anxiety. The United States was involved in a war of ideals with the Soviet Union. Americans worried that a real war could soon occur. Both the Soviet Union and the United States owned nuclear weapons. People were worried: *Would the bombs be used? Would new technology cause death and destruction?*

Anxious, Abstract Art

A new school of American art emerged from this blend of hope, wealth, and anxiety. It was known as abstract expressionism. Artists from this school felt that old styles of painting did not properly describe their world.

Abstract expressionists found unique ways to paint about their personal feelings. They no longer simply painted objects and figures that their viewers could recognize. Their paintings now featured wild experiments with colors, shapes, and patterns. The artists rarely made familiar images. However, their work did inspire genuine feelings.

Much of the American artwork created during the 1950s focused on capturing mood and emotion. To many critics, no artist of that time period expressed what it meant to be an individual more than Jackson Pollock.

The most famous artist of this period was Jackson Pollock. At this time, many artists chose to have their work tell a story. Pollock's art didn't tell stories, though. His pieces were deeply personal. Pollock became famous for splashing paint on his canvases. Sometimes he dripped paint across part of the canvas. Other times, he dipped a brush into a paint can and flung it across his artwork. His work responded to a changing culture. "The modern painter cannot express this age, the airplane, the atom bomb, the radio, in the old forms...of any

The American art scene is often attracted to what's new, bold, and pioneering. By 2003, Pollock's work was already being included in an exhibit honoring the "Classics of Modern Art."

other past culture," he said. "Each age finds its own technique."

Many Americans embraced the freedom this new school of art allowed. In 1949, *Life* magazine named Pollock "the greatest living painter in America." The work of Pollock and his peers came to represent the pioneering spirit of America.

Mark Rothko was another famous artist during this period. Rothko painted big blocks and fields of color on his canvases. One painting from 1953 shows a rectangle of magenta hovering over another rectangle, this one painted black. Rothko painted in thick layers. In fact, many of the brushes he used weren't the small kind bought at art stores. Instead, Rothko often bought brushes large and wide enough to paint houses!

The Birth of Pop

Not all artists were focused on personal expression. Some artists were beginning to focus on America's product-based culture. Many of them used popular images or objects

Did You Know?

POP ART ACTUALLY BEGAN IN ENGLAND. EARLY ENGLISH POP PIONEERS INCLUDE RICHARD HAMILTON, PETER BLAKE, AND EDUARDO PAOLOZZI. HOWEVER, POP SOON BECAME A MAJOR AMERICAN ART FORM.

Art by Robert Rauschenberg © Robert Rauschenberg Licensed by VAGA, New York

Robert Rauschenberg sits and smiles next to some of his paintings. Rauschenberg is also known for his work with other creative people, such as the famous dancer Trisha Brown.

in their art. However, they put their own creative spin on how they displayed the images.

Some of these American artists included Willem de Kooning, Robert Rauschenberg, and Jasper Johns. De Kooning painted a series of works with women as his subject. One woman is sitting in a field of grass. Her feet hover over a pool of water. This isn't a typical portrait, though. The women in de Kooning's paintings look angry. Their faces are cracked and split into sections. The features of their bodies are out of proportion.

Texan Rauschenberg found the abstract expressionists to be too serious. Rauschenberg liked to work everyday objects into his artwork. He used tennis balls, pillows—even a stuffed rooster! "A picture is more like the real world when it's made out of the real world," he once said. Johns focused on painting more familiar objects, such as maps and flags. These artists helped light the fuse for the pop art explosion that was about to hit the United States.

Pop artist Claes Oldenburg knew that Americans loved to buy things. Therefore, it made perfect sense to open a store that carried his own artwork on its shelves!

Eye-Popping Art

By the end of the 1950s, American art had made its stamp on the world. The nation's artists no longer felt like they were working in the shadow of Europe. At the same time, images that represented American culture were everywhere. From billboards of movie stars to ads selling soap or shoes, it was hard to avoid American products. Even when Americans weren't buying products, they were always in *contact* with products. Sometimes, Americans were watching TV commercials. Other times, they were hearing about products on the radio. Pop artists used common consumer items in their creations. They linked popular objects and images with fine art.

Shopping for a New Style

In December 1961, a strange store in New York City opened for business. Its owner was American pop artist Claes Oldenburg.

The shop was called *The Store*. It was both an art exhibit and a shop. Oldenburg created numerous plaster sculptures that looked like products. Some of his pieces were shaped like candy bars. Others looked like donuts and pastries.

The Store was a complex piece. It made fun of America's obsession with buying and consuming things. On the other hand, the items in *The Store* all carried a price tag. People could shop for art, too. Each time a customer bought one of Oldenburg's pieces, he replaced it with new "stock," or another piece of his unusual art.

In 1962, Oldenburg opened his "store" for a second time. This version featured all-new pieces. This time, he displayed soft-sculpture artwork. His newest creations were giant,

By 1963, Oldenburg had stopped using plaster in his sculptures. Pictured above is one of his first soft vinyl sculptures, *Giant BLT (Bacon, Lettuce, and Tomato Sandwich)*.

three-dimensional objects. Each object was something people bought, wore, ate, or used in some way. The pieces were made of vinyl or canvas. They were then stuffed with kapok. Kapok is the soft material often used to fill mattresses and sleeping bags.

One of Oldenburg's new pieces was a series of fur-covered ice cream bars. Another was a huge hamburger. This burger even featured a pickle on top! Oldenburg's *Soft Pay Telephone*

27

was another wild creation. The piece sags at the middle. It almost looks as though the phone has melted.

Many critics felt Oldenburg's work was pop art at its best. His creations forced viewers to take a second look at items they had begun to take for granted.

Fine Art Factory

Andy Warhol is probably the most famous American pop artist. Before he gained his great fame, Warhol drew pictures for big companies. He also designed store window displays. For Warhol, the line between money and art was often a blurry one.

Warhol's first paintings were done by hand. Soon after, though, he started using silk-screening techniques. Silk screening is a

Did You Know?

ANDY WARHOL'S FACTORY COULD MAKE UP TO 80 PAINTINGS IN ONE DAY.

Perhaps no other figure defines the American pop art movement like Andy Warhol (pictured here in 1987).

process in which artists squeeze ink through a stencil. This stencil is made from a silk screen. Silk screening allowed Warhol to create the same image many times.

Warhol's work focused on ways American culture mass-produced both goods and celebrities. Warhol explored how celebrities and products were used and then thrown away. His New York City studio was called The Factory. He paid his workers to mass-produce his art. This was similar to assembly

Warhol's sources of inspiration often came from images and products that people saw every day.

lines in real factories that made the same product, such as cars, over and over.

Most of Warhol's subjects were product logos or Hollywood stars. Warhol painted Campbell's soup cans, Coca-Cola bottles, and boxes of Brillo soap pads. In one painting, Warhol would often repeat the same image many times. His repeated images don't always look the same, though. In *Twenty-Five Colored Marilyns,* the first picture of Marilyn Monroe is stained with too much ink. Other times, the movie star's face appears faded or blotchy. Warhol actually meant for these kinds of "errors" to be in his work.

Pop art had become a success. As a result, the number of Americans selling and collecting art skyrocketed. When World War II ended, there were just two dozen major American art collectors. By 1970, there were over two thousand! In 1962, Warhol poked fun at the amount of money people were

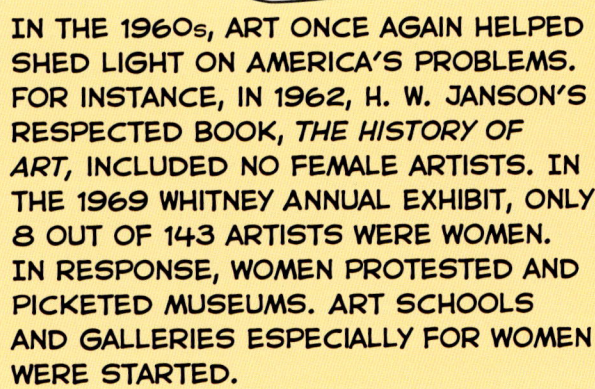

Fight for Your Rights!

IN THE 1960s, ART ONCE AGAIN HELPED SHED LIGHT ON AMERICA'S PROBLEMS. FOR INSTANCE, IN 1962, H. W. JANSON'S RESPECTED BOOK, *THE HISTORY OF ART,* INCLUDED NO FEMALE ARTISTS. IN THE 1969 WHITNEY ANNUAL EXHIBIT, ONLY 8 OUT OF 143 ARTISTS WERE WOMEN. IN RESPONSE, WOMEN PROTESTED AND PICKETED MUSEUMS. ART SCHOOLS AND GALLERIES ESPECIALLY FOR WOMEN WERE STARTED.

spending on art. One of his paintings was made up of 192 painted dollar bills. In other words, if you paid Warhol enough money, you could own his painting of money!

Not every painter was gaining success due to the pop art explosion. African-American artists were still struggling to get noticed. Some, such as Robert Colescott, blended popular images with images taken from African-American culture. One work by Colescott models itself after a beloved painting of George Washington. In the original, Washington stands proudly in a boat, crossing the Delaware River. Colescott replaced George Washington with famous African American George Washington Carver. This piece made a point that history books were ignoring the lives of African Americans.

Comic Art

Soda bottles or cans of soup didn't inspire Roy Lichtenstein's artwork. His inspiration came from a different source—comic books. Many of his paintings show violent scenes. *Whaam!* shows a fighter jet being blown

Most of Roy Lichtenstein's famous works, like *Whaam!*, were pulled straight from the funny pages.

apart by rockets. Because his paintings use only limited colors and quick sketches, the impact of the violence is not felt. Some critics felt that this was part of Lichtenstein's point.

Other paintings were based on romance comics. In the speech balloons, characters spoke dramatically. The character in *Hopeless* is a young blonde woman who is crying. In the picture, her balloon reads, "That's the way—it should have begun! But it's hopeless!" The woman in this painting is supposed to be depressed. Lichtenstein's distant style of painting, however, made it hard to care for the character.

Less than a hundred years ago, American cities paid artists to build gold statues of goddesses. These days, these same cities have embraced pop art. Standing beside Philadelphia's City Hall is Oldenburg's sculpture, *Clothespin*.

Chapter

Pop Art Echoes On

After the 1960s, pop artists began to shift their artwork's focus and form. Lichtenstein no longer based his paintings on comic strips. Warhol switched from making paintings to making films. Oldenburg's sculptures grew larger and larger. One of his wonderful pieces from this era looks like a giant, used match. *Extinguished Match* is made from foam and steel. The tip appears to be charred and black. The rest of the match is a tan blonde color that looks like wood. Of course, no one person could hold up *Extinguished Match*. The sculpture is 22 1/2 feet (6.9 meters) tall and nearly 8 feet (2.4 m) wide!

Pop artists continued to produce work through the 1960s and beyond. Meanwhile, a new group of artists was waiting to follow them. Some had rejected the style and attitude of pop art. Others carried on its lessons in surprising or humorous directions.

New Flavors of Pop

In the 1980s, artists who had already found fans and praise were making money. Those artists just starting out, though, struggled to survive. Some of these struggling artists used graffiti to showcase their work. They painted on buildings or sprayed the outside of subway trains. They continued doing this until the art world noticed them. Once the art world noticed these new artists, they praised them. Other people noticed, too. Only they weren't so happy. They were angry that public and private property was being used as "canvases."

Keith Haring was one of these new artists. Some critics felt that Haring's work shared some of Warhol's style. Haring painted bright colors and playful images. He had his cartoonlike work

In October 1986, Keith Haring was invited to paint his colorful and vibrant images on a very grim, concrete canvas—the Berlin Wall.

placed on greeting cards, T-shirts, and many other types of products which people could buy. In doing this, Haring allowed his work to reach a much wider audience.

Jean-Michel Basquiat was another pop-influenced artist. Basquiat's work often features wild images, as well as words that have been

The work of Jeff Koons celebrates rich and famous Americans like Michael Jackson. However, the more fans that Koons makes, the richer and more famous he becomes, as well.

scratched out. Warhol worked with Basquiat on a 1984 painting. The piece they did together poked fun at the idea that each artist must work alone. Both Haring and Basquiat became friends of Warhol.

Puppy Love

Jeff Koons reflects American culture in a playful way. One of his pieces is a porcelain sculpture of singer Michael Jackson and his pet chimpanzee, Bubbles. Both man and monkey have been painted gold. Still another sculp-

POP ART ECHOES ON

ture looks like a giant puppy. *Puppy* is 42 feet (12.8 m) tall. Its body is made of steel. Its coat, however, is covered in flowers instead of fur. It can hold up to seventy thousand plants. Koons said he wanted *Puppy* to be a symbol of "love, warmth, and happiness."

Koons loves popular American culture. He also enjoys his own celebrity status. "I want to be as big an art star as possible," he's said. "I like the idea of my work selling for a lot of money."

The Other Side

Other artists have responded to pop art in a different way. They seem to distrust big business and mass-produced culture. Barbara Kruger fits in with this group. Kruger works with billboard-sized images. Her pieces resemble modern ads. Instead of selling a product, however, Kruger uses her space to sell ideas. Her pieces comment on media and popular culture. Kruger uses phrases such as, "I Shop Therefore I Am." Some fans wondered if Kruger's messages were meant as jokes—or as warnings.

With her billboard-sized images and catchy phrases, Barbara Kruger has made the line between art and advertisement a very blurry one.

New Words

obsession (uhb-**sess**-shuhn) something that a person or people think about all the time

papier-mâché (**pay**-pur muh-**shay**) paper soaked in glue which can be molded before it hardens

silk screening (**silk skreen**-ing) a way of making art that involves pressing ink through a stencil

social realism (**soh**-shuhl **ree**-uhl-izm) art movement in the 1930s in which artists used their work to push for social change

stencil (**sten**-suhl) a piece of paper, plastic, or metal with a design cut out of it

sweatshop (**swet**-shop) a storefront where working conditions are very poor

technique (tek-**neek**) a method or way of doing something that requires skill

urinal (**yoor**-uhn-uhl) a fixture in a public bathroom used to hold liquid waste

For Further Reading

Bolton, Linda. *Andy Warhol.* New York: Scholastic Library Publishing, 2002.

Duggleby, John. *Story Painter: The Life of Jacob Lawrence.* San Francisco, CA: Chronicle Books, LLC, 1998.

Knapp, Ruthie, and Janice Lehmberg. *Off the Wall: Museum Guides for Kids: American Art.* Worcester, MA: Davis Publications, Inc., 1998.

Barnes, Rachel. *Abstract Expressionists.* Crystal Lake, IL: Heinemann Library, 2002.

Cook, Janet. *Understanding Modern Art.* Tulsa, OK: EDC Publishing, 1992.

Mason, Paul. *Pop Artists.* Crystal Lake, IL: Heinemann Library, 2002.

Resources

Organizations

Museum of Modern Art Queens
33rd Street at Queens Blvd.
Long Island City, Queens, NY
(212) 708-9400
www.moma.org

Smithsonian Institution
P.O. Box 37012
S.I. Building, Room 153, MRC 010
Washington, D.C. 20013-7012
(202) 357-2700
www.smithsonian.org

Whitney Museum of American Art
945 Madison Avenue
New York, NY 10021
1-800-WHITNEY
www.whitney.org

Resources

Web Sites
National Gallery of Art: Kids
www.nga.gov/kids/kids.html
Learn about art from around the world on this Web site.

PBS: Art: 21
www.pbs.org/art21/
This Web site has lots of information about twenty-first-century art and artists.

Smithsonian: Kids
http://www.hirshhorn.si.edu/education/interactive/flash.html
Create your own pop art sculpture using the interactive tools on this Web site.

City Museum
www.citymuseum.org
Some of this museum's exhibits are built from recycled and recovered objects. Take a virtual tour of the space on this Web site.

Index

A
abstract expressionism, 18
advertisements, 13
Ashcan School, 10

B
Basquiat, Jean-Michel, 37–38
Big Show, The, 11–12
billboard, 25
blotchy, 31

C
canvas, 19, 21, 27, 36
celebrity, 39
Colescott, Robert, 32
collectors, 31
consumer, 25

D
de Kooning, Willem, 23
Demuth, Charles, 14
Duchamp, Marcel, 10–13

E
Eight, The, 9–10

F
factories, 13–14, 30
Factory, The, 29
Ford, Henry, 14

G
graffiti, 36
Great Depression, 14–15

H
Haring, Keith, 36–38
Holzer, Jenny, 41

J
Johns, Jasper, 23

K
kapok, 27
Koons, Jeff, 38–39
Kruger, Barbara, 39

L
Lichtenstein, Roy, 32–33, 35

M
Marsh, Reginald, 14
mass-produced, 29, 39
Monroe, Marilyn, 5, 31
museum, 5–6

Index

N
New Deal, 15

O
obsession, 26
Oldenburg, Claes, 26–28, 35

P
paintings, 5–6, 10, 14, 18, 23, 28, 32–33, 35
Pearl Harbor, 17
photographs, 5
Pollock, Jackson, 19–20
pop art, 12–13, 23, 28, 31–32, 36, 39, 41

R
Rauschenberg, Robert, 23
Roosevelt, Franklin Delano, 15
Rothko, Mark, 21

S
sculptures, 5, 15, 26, 35
Segal, George, 7
Shahn, Ben, 15
Sheeler, Charles, 13
silk screening, 28–29
social realism, 14
stencil, 29
Store, The, 26
sweatshops, 15

T
technique, 20, 28

U
urinal, 11

W
Warhol, Andy, 28–32, 35–36, 38
World's Fair (1893), 6

About the Author
Jil Fine has studied art for several years. Her favorite subject is drawing seascapes of her sailboat, *Precious Waves*. She is currently working as a freelance children's book writer.